Let Freedom Ring

George Washington

by Kristin Thoennes Keller

Consultant:
Mary Thompson
Research Specialist
Mount Vernon Ladies' Association
Mount Vernon, Virginia

Bridgestone Books
an imprint of Capstone Press
Mankato, Minnesota

Bridgestone Books are published by Capstone Press
151 Good Counsel Drive • P.O. Box 669 • Mankato, Minnesota 56002
http://www.capstone-press.com

Printed in the United States of America

Library of Congress Cataloging-in-Publication Data
Thoennes Keller, Kristin.
    George Washington / by Kristin Thoennes Keller.
        p. cm. — (Let freedom ring)
    Includes bibliographical references and index.
    ISBN 0-7368-1034-X
    1. Washington, George, 1732–1799—Juvenile literature. 2. Presidents—United States—Biography—Juvenile literature. 3. Generals—United States—Biography—Juvenile literature. [1. Washington, George, 1732–1799. 2. Presidents.] I. Title. II. Series.
    E312.66 .T49 2002
    973.4′092—dc21
                           2001001145
                           CIP

Summary: Follows the life of revered leader George Washington. Covers Washington's childhood on a farm and his early lessons on being a gentleman to his experience in the French and Indian War, his military leadership in the Revolutionary War, and finally, his role as first President of the United States.

Editorial Credits
Rebecca Aldridge, editor; Kia Bielke, designer; Stacey Field, production designer; Deirdre Barton, photo researcher

Photo Credits
Stock Market/© David Pollack, cover; Michael Freedman 1994, gwart.com/gw, 5; Corbis, 6, 10, 42-43 (objects), 12, 21, 39; PhotoDisc, 6 (hatchet), 17, 42 (drum); Library of Congress, 9, 10; North Wind Picture Archive, 15, 29, 31, 35; Hulton/Getty Archive Photos, 17, 23, 25; Virginia Museum of Fine Arts, Richmond. Gift of Edgar William and Bernice Chrysler Garbisch. Ron Jennings/Virginia Museum of Fine Arts, 19; Stock Montage, 27; FPG International, 33; Courtesy of Mount Vernon Ladies' Association, 37; Unicorn Stock Photos, 40.

1   2   3   4   5   6   07   06   05   04   03   02

AEB 7777

Table of Contents

Chapter One

Early Life of a Great Leader

Most people know that George Washington was the first president of the United States. His face appears on postage stamps, money, and Mount Rushmore. Streets, colleges, rivers, cities, and even one state are named after him.

What some people do not know is that George was a great leader even before he became president. As general of the Continental Army, he led colonial troops to victory in the Revolutionary War (1775–1783).

George's Family

George was born February 22, 1732, in Westmoreland County, Virginia. His parents were Augustine, or Gus as he was called, and Mary. George was the first child from his father's second marriage. Gus's first wife had died, leaving him with two sons. They were George's older half brothers, Lawrence and Augustine, Jr., who was nicknamed Austin.

George Washington
was an important man.
Even today, more than
200 years after his death,
he is the subject of
artists' work.

The Real George Washington?

Most people have heard the story about George chopping down a cherry tree and then admitting it to his father. Historians agree that this story was made up by an early writer of George's life. The author tried to show George's honesty by creating the tale.

When George Washington was young
And full of energy,
He took his little hatchet
And chopped a cherry tree.

George's father made most of his money by growing tobacco to sell to Britain. The iron mine Gus owned added to his income.

When George was only 11 years old, Gus died after returning home ill from a trip to Britain. Gus left most of his property to Lawrence and Austin, but left Ferry Farm to George. The family lived in this home at the time. George also inherited 10 of his father's 49 African slaves and three town lots in Fredericksburg. However, he would not get these until he was 21.

George's Schooling

Lawrence and Austin had gone to expensive schools in Britain. However, Mary could not allow George to do the same. After Gus' death, there was not enough money. Mary also was protective of her children and wanted George to stay on the farm. So he attended a local school.

At school, George was a good student who did very well in math. He read English literature and the Bible and studied geography. He also was taught how to behave like a gentleman.

Formal schooling ended for George at age 14. Throughout his life, this lack of education made George feel unsure of himself. Most of the men he knew later in life had more formal education than George had.

Young George's Habits and Behavior

George liked rules and order. In fact, he copied more than 100 rules for good behavior from a book. This book prepared young noblemen for the life they were expected to lead.

George was an active boy. He liked playing billiards, which is similar to the game of pool today. He also hunted, fished, and played cards. Some historians say George enjoyed pretending he was a soldier like his brother Lawrence. George also enjoyed breaking in wild horses.

George was graceful and tall for his age. He became a good dancer and borrowed money from his mother for music lessons. Physical strength also was something George was known for. It helped him become a good wrestler and horseback rider.

Rules to Live By

Copying rules into a notebook was George's way of teaching himself to be a gentleman. Perhaps these rules also helped him learn to control his bad temper. Here are some of the rules for behavior that George noted.

In the presence of others, sing not to yourself with a humming noise nor drum with your fingers or feet.

If you cough, sneeze, sigh or yawn, do it not loud but privately.

Sleep not when others speak. Sit not when others stand. Speak not when you should hold your peace.

Turn not your back to others, especially in speaking.

Keep your nails clean and short, also your hands and teeth clean yet without showing any great concern for them.

Associate yourself with men of good quality if you esteem your own reputation . . . .

Kill no vermin [such] as fleas, lice, ticks, etc., in the sight of others.

Drink not nor talk with your mouth full.

George's First Job

George was interested in surveying, or recording land boundaries. The first piece of property that George surveyed was a turnip field at Mount Vernon. Lawrence had received this land upon his father's death.

When George was in his teens, he found his first job as a paid surveyor. Other jobs followed. Some were for the colonial government and many were for landowners.

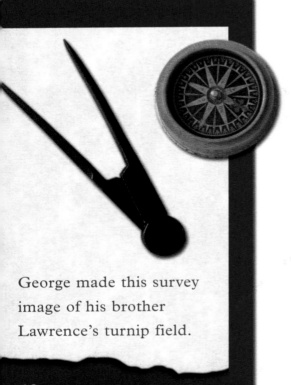

George made this survey image of his brother Lawrence's turnip field.

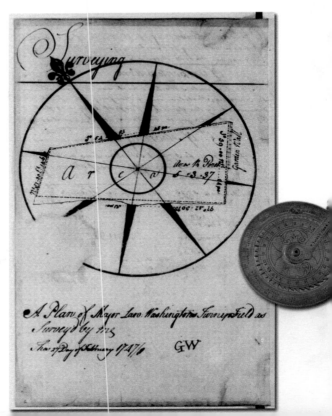

Illness in the Family

In the winter of 1751, Lawrence became sick with a lung disease called tuberculosis. George traveled with him to the island of Barbados. They hoped the warm weather would help Lawrence. While there, George caught a disease called smallpox. Many people died from this disease in the 1700s. George recovered and, like others who survived, was left with scars on his face.

George may have been lucky to get and survive smallpox when he did. Twenty-five years later, the disease killed many of his men during the Revolutionary War. But George never caught smallpox again.

Lawrence and George spent several months in Barbados, but Lawrence's condition did not improve. George left for Virginia to tell Lawrence's wife the news. Lawrence later sailed back to Virginia and died there in 1752. It was a sad loss for George. Because George and his mother did not get along well, he spent a lot of time with Lawrence. Losing Lawrence was like losing another father.

When Lawrence died, George was given Lawrence's position in the military, which included training Virginia's troops. The position paid enough for George to live on. When Lawrence's daughter died later, George inherited Mount Vernon and eight slaves. George had always loved Mount Vernon, and he lived there the rest of his life.

When George inherited Mount Vernon, the house had only four rooms on the first floor and three bedrooms on the second floor. Over the years, George made the house bigger and added many new rooms.

Diseases of the Revolution

Disease killed many people during the time of the Revolutionary War. Few doctors were formally trained to treat diseases. Most were self-taught or studied under another doctor. Only a few had training in Europe. Some of the most common diseases of the time included:

Dysentery: causes normally solid body waste to become runny and frequent (George had dysentery many times throughout his life).

Malaria: causes periods of chills and fever (George had malaria four times).

Scurvy: causes gums to become spongy and teeth to loosen; also causes bleeding into the skin.

Smallpox: causes skin to breakout with bumps that scar (George had smallpox only once).

Tuberculosis: causes lung problems (George had tuberculosis once).

Typhoid fever: causes fever, diarrhea (dysentery), headache, and stomach problems (George had typhoid fever once).

Yellow fever: causes fever, skin yellowing, and bleeding

Chapter Two

Starting the French and Indian War

Britain and France had been enemies for a long time. Both countries wanted control of America's western lands. French traders began building forts along the Ohio River, a move that concerned the British. Lieutenant Governor Robert Dinwiddie of Virginia wanted to warn the French that they should leave. Dinwiddie sent two men on this mission. When they both failed, Dinwiddie chose George for the job.

In 11 weeks, George traveled nearly 1,000 miles (1,600 kilometers). When he returned from the trip, George reported that the French refused to leave. Governor Dinwiddie made George lieutenant colonel in March 1754.

The French and Indian War

George was ordered to lead a troop of about 160 soldiers to a British post. This post was

George proved himself to
be an honorable, brave,
and clever military leader
during the French and
Indian War.

located along the Ohio River, where Pittsburgh stands today.

George found out that the French had taken over the post and renamed it Fort Duquesne. George and his troops set up their own camp. The British named it Fort Necessity. On May 28, 1754, George's spies saw a group of 30 French soldiers approaching Fort Necessity. George and a small troop attacked, killing the French commander. In a rainstorm, 700 angry French and American Indians attacked Fort Necessity.

After a day of fighting, George surrendered. His men were allowed to go free. However, the French gained control of the Ohio Territory. This was George's only record of surrender as a military commander. This small battle began the French and Indian War (1754–1763).

George Aids General Braddock

Several months after George returned from Fort Necessity, he quit the military. He was unhappy because British soldiers had not treated him with respect. Most British soldiers felt that they were more important than colonial soldiers like George.

In 1755, George rejoined the military to aid General Edward Braddock. Britain sent Braddock to help remove the French from the western areas of the British colonies. General Braddock had never fought in America. His troops wore bright red coats as they marched through the woods. The bright coats and the noise from fifes and drums concerned George. He felt the troops were announcing their arrival. George tried to warn Braddock that the French and the American Indians might attack unexpectedly. Braddock would not listen.

This actor in military dress plays a fife. Drummers and fife players kept time for British soldiers as they marched.

The French and the American Indians did make a surprise attack. As the British troops ran away, George bravely tried to stop them. George fought even though he was ill. He was so sick that he had pillows attached to his saddle to make riding more comfortable. Two horses were shot out from under George during the attack. Four bullets passed through his clothing and hat. Remarkably, the only officer not injured that day was George. Braddock, however, was shot in the lung and died.

News Spreads of George's Courage

Word of George's courage spread through the colonies. He was offered the job of defending Virginia from the French and the American Indians as colonel.

As leader, George made changes in the military's strategy. He had his troops use surprise methods. They wore clothing that stood out less than the bright red uniforms did. They no longer played fifes and drums.

The war lasted until 1763, when the British finally won. But George was not involved in the war that long. Late in 1758, he retired from military service and went home to Mount Vernon.

The Washingtons

Soon after George left the military, he married Martha Dandridge Custis. He had met Martha, a 27-year-old widow with two children, earlier in 1758. Martha's husband had left her well off when he died. She was the richest widow in Virginia.

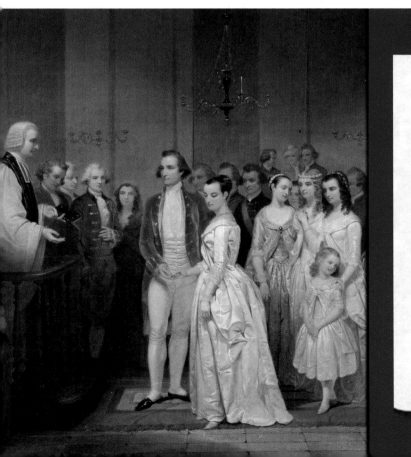

George and His Wife

When George asked Martha Dandridge Custis to marry him, they had spent a total of only 20 hours together. However, they had written many letters and learned about each other through friends.

The marriage, which took place on January 6, 1759, was a happy one. George helped to raise Martha's two children—John Parke and Martha Parke Custis.

The Washington family lived a full life at Mount Vernon. They entertained visitors and enjoyed fox hunting and dancing. They also liked to attend puppet shows and theater. George went to horse races and enjoyed playing card games for small amounts of money.

Keeping Busy

George was a hardworking farmer with a good head for business. He grew wheat and tobacco and experimented with many other crops. George raised animals that helped feed his workers and produced wool to make into clothing.

By 1774, George's life was peaceful but busy. As a member of the House of Burgesses, George helped make Virginia's laws.

He was elected many times to this governing body.
He also added on to and improved Mount Vernon.
Soon, George's life would become even busier and
less peaceful.

George had African slaves who worked on his farm. All the slaves
worked six days a week from sunup to sundown.

Chapter Three

The Continental Congress

After defeating France in 1763, Britain had many expenses. The country needed to pay back money it had borrowed to fight the war. Britain also needed soldiers to protect the colonies from American Indians. The British government wanted the colonies to pay for this protection with taxes. Colonists thought it was unfair to be taxed without any say in government.

The tea tax angered many colonists. In December 1773, in Boston, a group of colonists sneaked aboard British ships. They dumped the tea from the ships into the water. This act became known as the Boston Tea Party.

The Congress Meets

The Continental Congress met in Philadelphia on September 5, 1774. Representatives were present from each colony except Georgia. George was chosen to represent Virginia. The

In 1773, colonists disguised as American Indians dumped tea from a British ship into Boston Harbor. George did not approve of the Boston Tea Party. He understood the colonists' anger but did not like that they destroyed British property.

In His Own Words

In a letter to a friend, George wrote: "I think the Parliament [government] of Great Britain hath no more right to put their hands into my pocket, without my consent, than I have to put my hands in yours for money."

Congress discussed the colonists' concerns about British rule. At the time, George and his peers were not seeking independence from Britain. They just wanted to be treated like the British citizens who lived in Britain.

In March 1775, George was elected to represent Virginia at the second Continental Congress. However, before this meeting on May 10, 1775, the colonists had their first military encounter with the British. The colonists had formed small military groups called militias. Volunteer members of the militias were willing to protect the colonies from the British.

In April, British troops fought the colonial militia outside Boston at Lexington and Concord. The Second Continental Congress voted to help Boston's colonial troops.

At meetings, George wore his military uniform as a reminder of his military experience. He served on military committees, or groups, in Congress and offered to organize a military troop. Congress decided that one man was needed to serve as general and commander-in-chief of the colonial army. The Continental Congress chose George.

This document shows that the Continental Congress chose George to be general of the colonial army. George refused a salary, or payment, for this position. He asked only that his expenses be covered.

Chapter Four

Leader of the Revolution

George's role as military leader was challenging. Individual states did not send the supplies they were supposed to, even when ordered by Congress. George had trouble getting enough money for his troops from Congress. Often, he had to depend on poorly trained soldiers. Many soldiers signed up for only one year of service at a time.

The Declaration of Independence

On July 4, 1776, the Continental Congress approved the Declaration of Independence. The conflict between Britain and its American colonies had become a war for independence.

George was an important decisionmaker and leader of the time. However, his signature is not on the Declaration of Independence. At the time, George had just helped force the British out of Boston. He was moving his troops toward New York, where he thought the British would strike next.

George knew that taking the position as head of the military was risky. He knew that if he failed, he would probably be hanged as a traitor. But George believed in what he was doing.

Revolutionary War Facts

• By 1779, as many as one in seven Americans in Washington's army was African.

• By 1779, more Americans were fighting on the side of the British than alongside Washington. About one-third of Americans opposed the war.

Crossing the Delaware

George's troops were in New Jersey in the winter of 1776. The British Army's leader declared that his troops were done fighting for the season. George prepared for action. He planned to attack the enemy while they were sleeping on Christmas morning.

Through sleet and snow, George and his troops bravely crossed the Delaware River on Christmas Eve. While the enemy slept in their Trenton, New Jersey, camp, George and his troops attacked. They won the battle and went on to victory in Princeton, New Jersey, as well.

Loyalty to George

In October 1777, American General Horatio Gates accepted the surrender of the British at Saratoga, New York. This victory helped France decide to fight alongside the Americans. Some people thought Gates was responsible for the victory. They wanted him to replace George as military leader. But most members of Congress respected George too much and refused to consider this idea.

Crossing the freezing water of the Delaware River took George and his troops 14 hours.

George as Leader

George was a strategic leader. He planned and organized surprise attacks. Once, he had moved his army by night but left campfires burning to fool British spies. George even fooled the British into thinking that they were spying on him. Through spies he had placed in the British Army, George leaked stories about the size of his own army. So the British thought George's army was bigger than it really was.

Wintering at Valley Forge

George knew his troops needed a rest during the winter of 1777 and 1778. They set up quarters at Valley Forge, Pennsylvania, to watch the British.

Conditions were terrible. It was very cold, and soldiers did not have proper clothing or shoes. They left bloody footprints in the snow. Disease killed many men. Many other men left the army and returned to their own farms and homes.

Other soldiers trusted George and stayed while he tried to get food and supplies from Congress. Reportedly, some men boiled their shoes and ate them because there was so little food.

George's Disappointment in a Friend

Commander Benedict Arnold was exposed in 1780 as a traitor. He had been caught giving American plans to the British. Arnold became a leader in the British army and fought against George.

George was disappointed at Arnold's betrayal because they had been friends. When he read that Benedict Arnold was a traitor, George said, "Arnold has betrayed me. Who can I trust now?"

This building served as Washington's headquarters at Valley Forge.

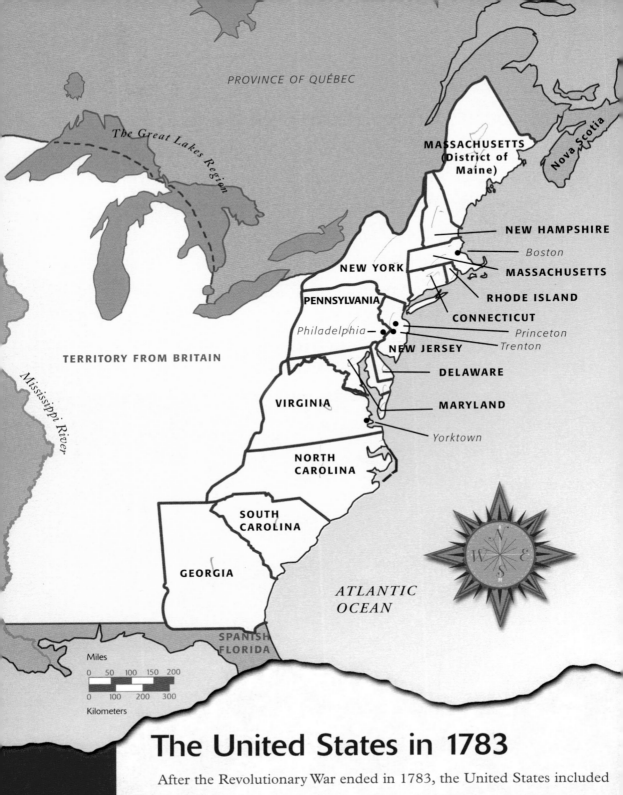

PROVINCE OF QUÉBEC

The Great Lakes Region

MASSACHUSETTS
(District of Maine)

Nova Scotia

NEW HAMPSHIRE

Boston

NEW YORK

MASSACHUSETTS

PENNSYLVANIA

RHODE ISLAND

CONNECTICUT

Philadelphia

Princeton

TERRITORY FROM BRITAIN

NEW JERSEY

Trenton

DELAWARE

Mississippi River

VIRGINIA

MARYLAND

Yorktown

NORTH
CAROLINA

SOUTH
CAROLINA

GEORGIA

ATLANTIC
OCEAN

N
W E
S

SPANISH
FLORIDA

Miles
0 50 100 150 200

0 100 200 300
Kilometers

The United States in 1783

After the Revolutionary War ended in 1783, the United States included

13 colonies and stretched west to the Mississippi River.

Victory at Yorktown

In 1781, George and the French allies pretended to prepare for an attack on British troops in New York. Instead, they headed south to Yorktown, Virginia. In October, British General Charles Cornwallis surrendered at Yorktown and ended the war.

Cornwallis refused to appear at the surrender ceremony at Yorktown. Instead, he sent his second in command. George therefore refused to accept the surrender himself and had his second in command accept.

George said good-bye to his officers in New York City. Many of the men cried as George hugged them. Congress thanked George for his achievements and offered the thanks of the country. By Christmas Eve, 1783, George was home with Martha at Mount Vernon. He was just past 50 years old.

This is the uniform George wore when he left the army in December 1783.

Chapter Five

The First President

After the war, George worried about the new country. The government was weak and paper money had no real value. There was no official army, and states were arguing with one another. George wanted to stay home at Mount Vernon, but he knew he had to help.

In May 1787, George went to the Constitutional Convention in Philadelphia. The purpose of this meeting was to rewrite the Articles of Confederation that guided the current American government. George's peers elected him president of the Convention because they knew he would stay calm and be fair. When the Convention ended, the attendees had created the Constitution of the United States.

As president of the Constitutional Convention, George said little in the debate. However, listening carefully and patiently, he decided who could speak and for how long.

George's Goals as President

1) To preserve the government that represented the people of the country

2) To steady the country's finances by raising taxes and settling debts

3) To improve relations with Britain and the rest of Europe

4) To develop the frontier and make treaties with American Indians

Becoming President

One of the topics discussed at the Convention was a presidency for the new country. In 1789, George was elected the first President of the United States, without campaigning.

As George rode to New York for his inauguration, people came out to greet him. They cheered as he took the oath of office at this formal ceremony.

Strengthening the Country

During George's presidency, the country became stronger, and the dollar gained value. The Bill of

Rights became law, and relations with American Indians improved.

George signed treaties to keep the nation out of war. He did not want to side with anyone, especially France or Britain. He thought the United States needed several years of peace in order to grow and become rich. Then, the country could defend itself.

George wanted to return to Mount Vernon and farm after the first four years of his presidency. But he agreed to another four years and was again elected without opposition.

George's Presidency Ends

George did not want to serve a third term. He wanted to show the people that a president was not elected for a lifetime. He did not want to rule like a king. In

Those Famous Teeth

John Adams claimed that George believed he lost his teeth by cracking walnuts in his mouth. By the time he was president, George had only one tooth left. George had false teeth made. These teeth were not made of wood like many people believe. They were made of cow's teeth, human teeth, and elephant ivory. They were set in a lead base with springs that let him open and close his mouth. The teeth fit poorly and caused him constant pain. They also changed the shape of his mouth.

Washington, D.C.

During his presidency, George picked the final site for the United States government. He visited the new city, which was just being built along the Potomac River. On September 18, 1793, he laid the cornerstone of the United States Capitol building.

March 1797, George left politics and returned to Mount Vernon.

His days at Mount Vernon were peaceful. George enjoyed riding his horses around the fields. He wrote many letters and often read the newspaper aloud to Martha. George continued to make repairs at Mount Vernon. He had many visitors, and some strangers even stopped by without invitation.

A Great Leader Dies

On a snowy December day in 1799, George returned wet after riding his horse. He ate dinner in his wet clothes. He was probably sick before his ride. That evening, he had a sore throat. During the night, he had trouble breathing. Unfortunately, medicine did not help.

The next day, three doctors came. They tried various cures, including a mixture of molasses, butter, and vinegar. They also drew blood from his body, a common practice at the time.

Famous artists wanted to paint the first president of the United States. George agreed to pose for portraits.

As George became weaker, he seemed to know he was dying. He looked over his will, making sure that his slaves would be given their freedom. He died December 14, at 10:00 at night with Martha by his side. He was 67 years old. Martha died in 1802. George and Martha are buried in the family tomb at Mount Vernon.

On his deathbed (pictured here), George said to those around him: "I find I am going, my breath can not last long....Doctor, I die hard; but I am not afraid to go...."

Trying to Bring Back the Dead

After George died, one doctor wanted to try to bring him back to life. This doctor planned to put the body in cold water, then lay it in blankets and warm it further by rubbing it. Then he wanted to cut open a passage in the throat to allow airflow into the lungs. Finally, he wanted to give George the blood of a lamb. Others present did not allow this.

What George Left Behind

George spent much of his life serving his country. He applied the leadership skills he learned in the military to his presidency. Other world leaders came to respect and trust George. France considered him a friend. Britain came to respect George, even though he was a former enemy.

George's influence on the United States is still felt. But perhaps the most important part of his legacy is that he chose not to become king. With the respect people had for George and the power he was given, he easily could have. Instead, he served two terms as president, then left politics for a quiet life at Mount Vernon.

TIMELINE

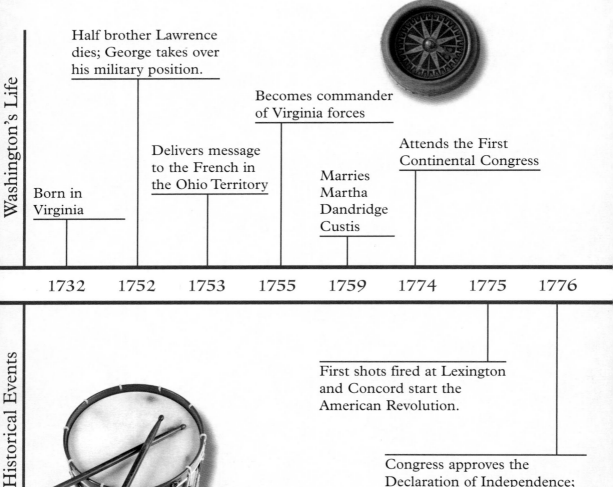

Washington's Life

Half brother Lawrence dies; George takes over his military position.

Becomes commander of Virginia forces

Delivers message to the French in the Ohio Territory

Attends the First Continental Congress

Born in Virginia

Marries Martha Dandridge Custis

| 1732 | 1752 | 1753 | 1755 | 1759 | 1774 | 1775 | 1776 |

Historical Events

First shots fired at Lexington and Concord start the American Revolution.

Congress approves the Declaration of Independence; George and his troops have victory at Trenton, New Jersey.

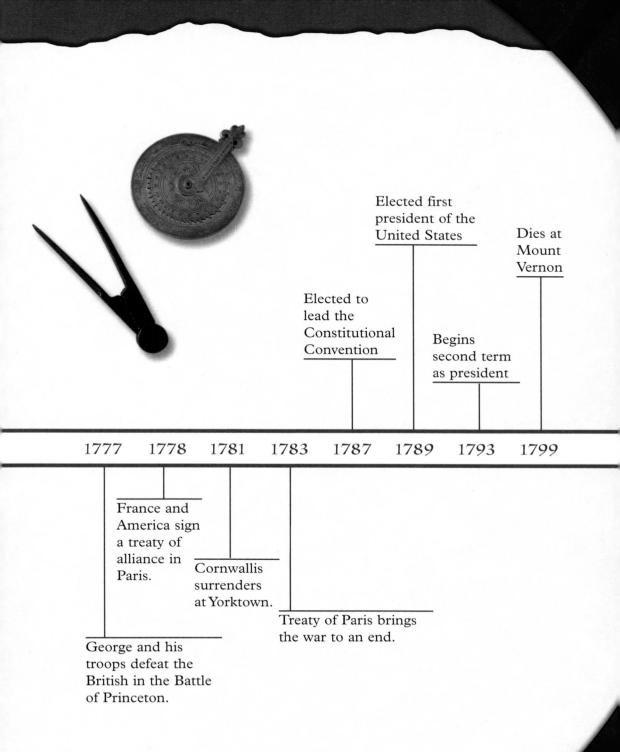

Elected first
president of the
United States

Dies at
Mount
Vernon

Elected to
lead the
Constitutional
Convention

Begins
second term
as president

1777   1778   1781   1783   1787   1789   1793   1799

France and
America sign
a treaty of
alliance in
Paris.

Cornwallis
surrenders
at Yorktown.

George and his
troops defeat the
British in the Battle
of Princeton.

Treaty of Paris brings
the war to an end.

Glossary

ally (AL-eye)—a person or country that gives support to another

colony (KOL-uh-nee)—an area of land and water settled and governed by a distant country

defeat (di-FEET)—to beat someone in a war or competition

inaugurate (in-AW-gyur-rate)—to swear an official into public office with a formal ceremony

militia (muh-lish-uh)—a group of citizens who are trained to fight but serve only in times of emergency

Parliament (PAR-luh-muhnt)—a political group that makes the laws in Britain

smallpox (SMAWL-poks)—a disease that spreads easily from person to person, causing chills, fever, and pimples that scar; smallpox often causes death.

strategy (STRAT-uh-jee)—a plan for winning a military battle or achieving a goal

surveyor (sur-VAY-uhr)—a person who measures land boundaries

tax (TAKS)—money that people and businesses must pay to support a government

treason (TREE-zuhn)—the crime of betraying one's country by spying for or helping another country

widow (WID-oh)—a woman whose husband has died

For Further Reading

Collier, Christopher, and James Lincoln Collier. *The American Revolution, 1763–1783*. New York, Benchmark Books, 1998.

George-Isms: The 110 Rules George Washington Wrote When He Was 14 and Lived by All His Life. New York: Atheneum Books for Young Readers, 2000.

Harness, Cheryl. *George Washington*. Washington, D.C.: National Geographic Society, 2000.

Heilbroner, Joan, and Stephen Marchesi. *Meet George Washington*. New York: Random House, 2001.

Peacock, Louise. *Crossing the Delaware: A History in Many Voices*. New York: Atheneum, 1998.

Todd, Anne. *The Revolutionary War*. America Goes to War. Mankato, Minn.: Capstone Books, 2001.

Places of Interest

Fort Necessity National Battlefield
One Washington Parkway
Farmington, PA 15437
http://www.nps.gov/fone
See where George lost the first battle of the French and Indian War.

The Library of Congress Manuscript Reading Room
Room LM101, James Madison Building
101 Independence Avenue Southeast
Washington, D.C. 20540-4680
http://www.loc.gov/rr/mss
Has a collection of documents related to George.

Mount Vernon
Mount Vernon Ladies' Association
P.O. Box 110
Mount Vernon, VA 22121
http://www.mountvernon.org
The home of George and Martha

Valley Forge National Historic Park
P.O. Box 953
Valley Forge, PA 19482-0953
http://www.nps.gov/vafo
The place George and his men camped during the winter of 1777 and 1778

Washington Crossing Historic Park
P.O. Box 103
Washington Crossing, PA 18977
http://www.spiritof76.net/wchp
Park dedicated to the crossing of the Delaware River by George and his troops

Washington Monument
15th Street Northwest at Constitution Avenue
Washington, D.C.
http://www.nps.gov/wamo/home.htm
This landmark was built to honor the first U.S. president

Internet Sites

George and Martha Washington: Portraits from the Presidential Years
http://www.npg.si.edu/exh/gw
A display of various images of George and Martha

Liberty! The American Revolution
http://www.pbs.org/ktca/liberty
Contains a variety of information on the American Revolution

Library of Congress American Memory Project
http://memory.loc.gov/ammem/gwhtml/gwhome.html
Access to the George Washington papers at the Library of Congress

Mount Vernon
http://www.mountvernon.org
Provides information on George, his home, and his life as a farmer

Index